MY ONLY HOME

OTHER POETRY *by* FREYA MANFRED

A Goldenrod Will Grow
Yellow Squash Woman
American Roads
Flesh and Blood

MEMOIR

Frederick Manfred: A Daughter Remembers

FREYA MANFRED

MY ONLY HOME

POEMS

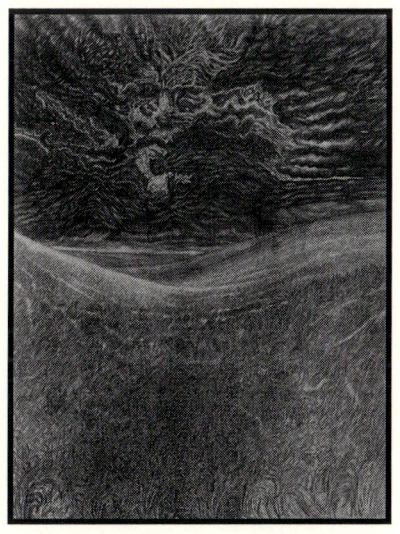

RED DRAGONFLY PRESS

Northfield - 2003 - Minnesota

Copyright © 2003 by Freya Manfred

ISBN 1-890193-30-5

This book is set in Minion Pro

Red Dragonfly Press
307 Oxford Street
Northfield, MN 55057

For information about Red Dragonfly Press
please visit our website:
www.reddragonflypress.org

❡ CONTENTS

7   On Attachment
8   The Horror Of The World Around

GIVING BIRTH

11 Giving Birth
12 Tidal Wave
13 Valley
14 Nightmare
15 I Don't Have A Philosophy
16 The Invalid Speaks
17 To My Son, Laughing In His Sleep
18 The Lust Of Mothers For Their Sons
19 Mother Fear
20 Like You Used To, Father
21 Men's Tears
22 My Sons In Their Flowered Caps
23 Husband, Two Kids, And A Station Wagon
24 My Father By The Fire
26 Words About Death
27 Green Pear Tree In September
28 When My Dead Father Visits
29 What Other Life?
30 Ear
31 Hair

33	Toes
34	Husband
35	The Husband Speaks Of Menopause
36	The Wife Speaks Of Menopause
37	Asses
39	My Grandmother's Ass
40	Blue Hair Blues
42	Lilacs
44	Grass
46	A Body Heals
47	Message From The Right Brain
49	Heart

THE LAKE THAT WHISPERS TO ITSELF

53	Spring
63	Summer
81	Fall
91	Winter

acknowledgments

❡ ILLUSTRATIONS

cover	Bly Pope, "Pink Flowers"
titlepage	Rowan Pope, "Prairie With Storm"
53	Bly Pope, "Moth"
63	Rowan Pope, detail from "Garden"
81	Rowan Pope, detail from "Old Man"
91	Bly Pope, "Snow Trees"

Dedicated to my two favorite places to swim:

Willard Pond, New Hampshire
&
Christmas Lake, Minnesota

ON ATTACHMENT

Whether you have a father or a mother
doesn't matter.
Where you want to feel most at home
is with the stars,
and the emptiness that holds them,

your brain dividing
branching,
until its smallest extremity
receives the frail signals
coming toward you from a black horizon:

And you are flooded with the knowledge
that you are not a wife,
or a mother,
neither sick, nor well, nor anyone's ghost.
You are not a writer or a plumber.

You are what is left when these others
vanish: someone
most people will never meet:
the one mortals speak of
when they whisper of gods.

But you're no god, or any such word,
only brimming with joy,
facing the dark.
And the sweetness of being attached to no one
will always be with you.

for Olga Naud

THE HORROR OF THE WORLD AROUND

If you have no warm room
where you can sit and stare into a tea cup,
if no grim women divorced from their bodies
arrive at your door with underarm Bibles, crooning,
"Are you longing for a power
greater and wiser than yourself?",
if no one leaves notes on your windshield saying,
"We'll take this Chevy off your hands for a hundred,"
then you are left
with the horror of the world around.
You are at war, marching into enemy territory,
taking lives or letting your life be taken.
Women stand at their back doors
and avert their eyes from you.
Every town looks the same:
freeways, truck stops, no trespassing.
You're lucky to find a cave in a large tree
where you can crouch when it rains,
or a refrigerator box
where you can cut a small hole and peer out
like when you were a child in your own back yard,
and at sunset, mother called you home.

GIVING BIRTH

Mom, if I kiss a flower, will that make it grow bigger?

—Rowan Pope, age 5

GIVING BIRTH

Snow flails the wings of the house.
My husband and two children labor through a winter flu.
Up all night, I think of my brother, ill,
my sister, lost.

My aging parents stand in the front yard,
giant frosted oaks glowing in the blizzard's eerie light
as if their birth star
were streaming back to take them home.

I'm the only parent left,
and I'm afraid the burden will bury me, no use reasoning.
I've strained since childhood under storms and sicknesses
I cannot dream of ending.

What can I do?
What have I ever done,
for the ones I love best?

I must lie down, and think of giving birth,
how it overtakes the mother and the child,
obliterates and makes them whole,
just when they would have gone on forever
in the half dark of each others' wombs.

TIDAL WAVE

How will I swim
with both arms
holding twin sons?

Should I save
the soft-hearted boy
born with one raised fist?

Or the boy
who first saw the stars
beyond my face?

Over and over
I choose them both,
stroking toward the light.

Why do I feel satisfied
riding the curve of my death
and theirs?

I am doing what I can
even if it is never
enough.

VALLEY

I rise with the morning wind
and push my two sons in their stroller
to the playground.

In the waving grass
my breasts are buoys.
I ferry little wanderers from shore to shore.

The blue mountain in the distance
reminds me of the valley
on the other side

where dust lies quiet as a soul,
rich as the forest
which will spring from it.

I am sitting
in the shade my children make
when they insist I am their tree.

NIGHTMARE

I'm leaving the house
to meet my husband's plane.
My sons stand on the doorstep,
shouting goodbye.
As I turn to wave,
the bomb hits
west of Plymouth,
dissolving the oaks, pines and lilacs
of central Minnesota,
overtaking me at the instant
my husband flies toward us,
dwarf-high in the jet.
As the fire storm inscribes itself
upon the Minnesota River Valley,
last shaped by the Ice Age,
I stretch one arm back toward my sons,
the other raised into the sky.
I don't have time to wonder if the plane
will find a place to land in hell.

I DON'T HAVE A PHILOSOPHY

> Life has never been able to believe in death.
> —Carl Jung

Day after day my best friend dies
with a reluctant grace
I doubt I could own.
Months go by,
but I don't adjust to the facts.

I love to swim
and usually enjoy my dinner.
I go to bed blessing the hairs
that rise on my scalp during good music.
But sometimes my arms fall empty beside me.
I'm so lonely, so helpless,
I push my children away.

I hope some day
a philosophy will whisper itself to me,
something I read, or heard, but never felt—
until emptiness entered and wrote itself
in my hollow places,
where no one but the loser
suspects the reason why we live, or die,
and only the lost
can bear back into the light
the right wordless word
for those who carry on.

THE INVALID SPEAKS

Something beyond
lying here,

something wide
and embracing
as the sky,

something I may only
be dreaming of,

expects me.

I am
becoming
myself.

This is not death,
but it feels like death,

as if I were pregnant
with space.

TO MY SON, LAUGHING IN HIS SLEEP

Since he was a baby
I have awakened in the night
startled
by the bell-sweet sound
of his laugh.
I am propelled,
cold, knees creaking,
across the cluttered floor
to his bed,
my face above his face:
yes, he is asleep,
and smiling.

Back in my bed I hear again
his high warble.
How I envy this boy
who is not mine,
who was never mine.
How I praise him
for making everything in the world right
for one moment.

THE LUST OF MOTHERS FOR THEIR SONS

No wonder ancient fathers took their sons
from the dusky, hardworking mothers,
and popped them into kiva ovens
for private male ceremonies.
But it was too late:
the rosy lust of the mothers
already colored their sunset and their dawn.
I'm talking about pure mother lust,
strong women who fall in love
with their sons' outstretched arms
before those arms become oak branches
sprouting from plowshare shoulders.
I'm talking about blameless male babies
who share their mothers' flowering bodies
for nine dream-filled months
until the bag of waters breaks,
and mother and son blink for the first time
at the overwhelming beauty of each other:
the thunderclap of recognition
when the world enters,
and all dreams are possible,
and at an end.

MOTHER FEAR

Her joy places soft cheeses in my mouth,
and her sadness cuts off the light around my body.
All her fears are mine, even the fear of what remains
when fear is gone. But I'm grown now,
and there's more shape to the face
that must face her, and some understanding
of the simple awe we both felt as I emerged,
tiny and clinging, and any attack took my lifeblood with hers.

I remember the day when I stumbled outside,
no longer pressed like a moon to her warm stomach,
and I felt in my chest the glow that comes just before sunrise,
and the sky—without a navel—blessing me!
Let me explore my everlasting mother as I would the earth,
naming what I find, even of myself: which is to let go,
knowing I will fall, keeping in heart which way is up,
the only way to fall, again and again:

as underwater divers unhand all empty and treasure ships
and drop upward toward their personal breath
waiting at the invisible line
where sky and sea meet.

LIKE YOU USED TO, FATHER

Why won't you sit on the porch, father,
and talk with me
like you used to?

I left my husband,
beside me every night,
and came all the way from California to see you.

I have questions:
how you and mother parted,
why you moved west, and rarely saw old friends.

But you list awards, appointments,
prospective ball games
to catch on TV.

In mid summer
I walk up to my knees in snow
toward your unfinished house.

I wake and cry for my husband, who dotes on me
when I bake bread and read Proust,
the way you used to dote on me.

I know I've substituted a younger man for you,
one who might not have to say goodbye
so soon.

But I still love you,
the way you can't stop loving
the one you know as me.

So come out to the porch, father,
and talk with me,
like you used to.

MEN'S TEARS

Every day since school began
our ten year old son bursts into tears:
"My bike is scratched! My cat is hurt!"
He pushes away our hugs, and weeps,
standing, sitting, lying in the leaves,
the great head with zinnia-petaled hair
bowed over the heaving chest.
Helpless, hopeless, wave after wave,
he weeps until he's done.
It's hard for us to listen,
but we say to each other,
"Why shouldn't a boy cry?"
Please God, why shouldn't a man?
Why shouldn't all the men in the world
lie down and cry, feet dangling,
knuckles rubbing their wet faces.
Let them stop working, stop traveling, stop talking,
and sit, in the daylight, in the dark,
in the woods and cities and deserts,
and cry, sobs filling the sky,
inhalations flooding their lungs
with other men's exhalations,
connecting them together,
their bodies becoming one with rivers, lakes and seas:
while we sisters, mothers, and grandmothers
crouch down beside them, praying,
our bodies feeling their pain
as we do when our small sons cry:
sweet and strong, these men and nations,
bold enough to weep men's tears.

MY SONS IN THEIR FLOWERED CAPS

Out on the muddy April fields
they fling a baseball back and forth,
mocking and cajoling each other
in victory and defeat.

Today for the first time
I smelled their salty half-man sweat,
shocking as a timber wolf's footprint
in Boundary Waters snow.

But they chose their flowered caps
from the women's hat rack, not the men's,
charmed by the tropical colors,
the delicate bird and flower shapes.

Long may my sons in their flowered caps
bloom on the baseball fields of men,
wave their bats and grin white-fanged
into the pitcher's evil eye.

HUSBAND, TWO KIDS, AND A STATION WAGON

In my fantasy I'm strolling
along a lake in Minnesota.
I'm fifty, and beautiful,
edgy with a longing
that used to flare only in dreams.

Along comes Reid in his yellow pickup.
Reid, who hasn't seen me in thirty years,
is a stranger to his wife and friends,
and has daydreams in which I appear,
a familiar shape against the shining lake.

Reid and I drive all day across the prairie,
not saying much,
though he talks far more than he used to,
and I no longer pretend to understand.
I'm tired. I've worked hard
doing everything a person should.
Now I stroke his brown fingers
and lift them to my face.
I tell myself I can't chuck my real life.
I never have.

Except you can't kill a vision cooked up by two people
feeling alien to the world.
It's another kind of love,
not as fatal as therapists and best friends
would have you believe.

Besides, maybe the rest of the world is dead.
I don't want them dead,
but I've rarely been so happy—
and I can do this anytime
all by myself.

MY FATHER BY THE FIRE

He's eighty-two.
He splits and hauls the logs
and sets the fire himself:
first crumpled newspaper, stacked like baseballs,
next the kindling, two years dry,
and then the first log—pine is good—set far back,
with a second pine in front of it
and three oak logs on top, spaced to leave room for air;
then open the flue so the wood catches fire,
led by a thin trail of smoke fleeing to the sky.
Or, did his eyes start the fire without matches—
those bolts of blue lightning
in the old white thunder head?

His garden-stained pants hang from his bony knees,
and he's given up trying to straighten his back
even after he stands: bones, flesh, skin, hair,
worn thin by rivers in the sky.

He forgets what we said last week,
his memory a stone
that holds and releases the sun's heat
one day at a time.

If he goes, I'm wind.
I'm on the road again,
no more blue coffee cups on a homemade table.
I'll be traveling a long way for a laugh.

If he goes, will I remember how to make a fire?

Throbbing red coals beckon us
into the fertile black, green, and yellow forest,
where wild animals open their blazing lava eyes,

flex their claws, spit, lash their tails—
each fire laid exactly the same,
each aroused from slumber with one match,
saying everything that matters
to the father and his daughter:
we are crouched together in the wild storm,
but we are warm—and we are home.

WORDS ABOUT DEATH

I have always had words.
But for the moment of death
I have no words.

Even for my father's death,
and how I miss him.
No words.

The only person who might have
something true to say
is the dead man,
who has come back into this bed
with his hands crossed over his chest,
and his mouth closed forever.

Come back from the place he went
when words left us both,
and he followed.

GREEN PEAR TREE IN SEPTEMBER

On a hill overlooking the Rock River
my father's pear tree shimmers,
in perfect peace,
covered with hundreds of ripe pears
with pert tops, plump bottoms,
and long curved leaves.
Until the green-haloed tree
rose up and sang hello,
I had forgotten...
He planted it twelve years ago,
when he was seventy-three,
so that in September
he could stroll down
with the sound of the crickets
rising and falling around him,
and stand, naked to the waist,
slightly bent, sucking juice
from a ripe pear.

WHEN MY DEAD FATHER VISITS

When my dead father visits,
he speaks in a voice as familiar
as the clear stream below my childhood home.
Sometimes a woman accompanies him
with two children, a girl and a boy.
Sometimes he drives an ancient car,
and finds his way better than I can
through labyrinthic city streets.

When I ask what it's like to be dead,
he cries, "What do you mean, *dead*?
I'm very much alive, busy all day long!"

Sometimes I tell my children
about their grandfather's visits.
I tell them my dreams,
deeper than memory.
I tell them I'm grateful to talk
with the dead one who is not dead.
Because of him
I've come to love the living more.

WHAT OTHER LIFE?

Do you think I have the guts or heart
to pack my bag, gas my old car
and live alone in a strange hotel
on a turnpike in New Jersey?
Abandon a thousand bacon and egg breakfasts
floating on grease-filmed dishes,
two thousand knee bends picking up baseballs,
tennis shoes, kleenex, toilet paper, gum.
I'm no slick mermaid clinging to a rock in the sea—
and now, as the tide ebbs, I'm afraid
I'll be marooned on this beach,
scrutinized daily by merciless teenage eyes:
"Mom, do you have to talk so loud?"
"There's something gross on your lip!"
"Why are you holding Dad's hand?"
"What's that thing you're wearing?"
"Leave us alone!"
"Get out!"
"Go away!"
"Get a life!"
No, I won't! I'm your mother.
I want one more summer morning,
overflowing with chores before the sun's up,
where for one glorious moment
I stand on the porch
with my empty tea cup in one hand,
and have no need to fill it up again.

EAR

A squirrel cracks walnuts on the roof,
crickets sing in the swamp,
zinnias in a blue vase sigh.
I lie flat, hands forgotten, feet under a blanket,
no phone calls, no doorbells, no TV,
no jewelry knocking against my body,
no one to call me daughter,
sister,
mother,
or wife.

Call me newborn,
soft flower,
or ear.

Let me hear
the silence
that says what I want to say.

Let me rise from this civil grave
and speak one true word to my children
in this deafening age.

HAIR

I'll never forget
the first time Gramma Shorba
reached into her grey hair and unwound
her dead mother's brown hairpiece
till it fell into my hand.
"It's called a rat, honey.
Would you like to comb the tangles out?"
I was seven.
I held it by two fingers
as if it were half alive.
"Gramma, aren't you scared
Great-gramma will rise
from her grave at midnight
to snatch back her hair?"
"My stars, girl, if she does,
I hope she'll take me with her!"
"Gramma!"
"Because I'm lonely,
too lonely for this world."

My best friend, Diane Pond, whose hair
was the same shiny brown as Gramma's rat,
said my red hair was proof I was a liar
who would lead a lonely, tempestuous life
no man could share.
But one night I trimmed the sails of a fallen elm
and blew down the Mississippi to the sea
where I found a handsome prince
who would love me forever.
I don't treat him the way Gramma or Diane
told me to treat a man;
but in the first grey of every dawn

I'm thankful his face emerges
from the dark bed beside me,
as the sun rises—
its hair aflame, aflame.

TOES

A woman lost both big toes
in an accident;
to her it was as if
the two trees shading her house
were cut down.
Her tongue lay in mourning
in the vault of her mouth.
Her shins fought without compromise.
She could no longer bring herself
to eat with spoons,
and her forks matched her feet.
Sex with her husband
was like being called out at third
when she expected to slide home safe.
When he left her to marry
a twelve-toed cheerleader,
she retired to a hot tub
to suck her thumbs and die.
Her gardener buried her
beneath the Brussels sprouts
seventy-two toes under.

HUSBAND

Tonight the cat will take Tom's place in bed,
purring behind my knees,
and my sons will somersault
into my morning dreams.

Tom is flying in a plane over the Rockies.
Beyond my body's imagination,
he becomes every loss, every goodbye,
all I have and all I have given up,
from childhood on,
in too many blameless seasons of abandonment.

It's not wrong to love this way.
We share more than most people allow themselves
amid the daily pittances of life.
And the pain when he's absent
comes more to the child I harbor
than to the woman I've become.

With Tom, I'm a warm river
where every water lily flowers
with the white tongues of angels
in the only heaven there is:
when two people, after time apart,
ease their bodies together,
and claim their right to dream.

THE HUSBAND SPEAKS OF MENOPAUSE

She kisses my shaving cream ears,
and half an hour later
throws a loaf of bread across the room.
She hates to cook and clean,
and wants to do nothing but grow flowers,
tuck in seeds, water, weed,
sprinkle petals in our food.
On summer nights she crouches behind the tiger lilies,
eyes wild, clawing the dirt
until a fountain of nasturtiums sprouts.
When I try to cast my old loving spell on her,
she cackles, hops on her purple bergamot broom,
and soars into a white rose moon,
a dark, distant figure,
moving at an immense speed.

THE WIFE SPEAKS OF MENOPAUSE

I want him to drive slower.
I want him to keep our fire insurance up to date.
I want the butter out, the ketchup in,
the front door locked at night.
My wants lumber through our house, become mere wishes,
then die and fly to heaven unfulfilled,
until one morning I rise from sleep, screaming,
my sharp breasts pointed at his black unlistening heart.
He forgot to buy milk.
That's it, our marriage is over—
the man didn't remember the milk!
His face turns curd white.
With shaking paws, like Pooh Bear,
he offers me his last pot of honey.
He has saved me from extinction.
He's afraid of me.

Someone has to be.

ASSES

Whether or not I inherited my flat one
from my father or mother
was the source of intense argument—insane!—
because you couldn't rest even one beer can
on Mom's or Dad's.
The word "buttock" didn't apply to us.

Now I believe
the bigger the better:
something to steady you, hold down the fort,
a cubby for babies, a slide for school kids,
a football lineman's center of gravity.
I'm speaking of those big ones
like dollops of bread dough,
like a horse's hindquarters,
like the ones some waitresses in Nebraska
turn in your direction
after they serve the burgers;
those giant gumdrops,
those chestnuts, slick and fat;
they give me such a sense of security,
combined with a lust for hugs and kisses.
Such an ass could keep you warm
through the worst snowstorm;
it could save you from drowning,
and float you home like a barrel over Niagara;
it could fix the VCR
and figure out the income taxes;
or if all else failed and there was
nothing left but to face death in the eye,
such an ass could install itself
in a chair as wide and warm as Christmas
and sing, "Rock of ages, cleft for me,
let me hide myself in thee..."

That's what God must have meant
when he whispered that song
into the ear of a Lutheran organ player:
how much we all need one of those powerful
never-say-die, adult asses
to depend upon
in this Vale of Tears.

MY GRANDMOTHER'S ASS

My grandmother's bighearted ass
puddled over the kitchen stool
while she washed dishes.
I crouched beneath her flowered dress
and tickled her bunions.
She was the one person in our house
you could always tease,
because she was full of rhymes and sayings,
like "Willie Willie Wiener, backhouse cleaner,"
and "A rolling stone gathers no moss."
She'd weep rivers with you.
And when you were frightened
she'd bump into every piece of furniture
in an anxious dance to save you from yourself.
But best of all was how she'd listen
when you spoke, really hear you,
instead of saying, "Talk to you later,
when I finish *The New York Times*."
Plus, she couldn't run upstairs and punish us
every time she heard something break,
or squeeze herself through the culvert
we followed into the dark and scary woods.
Yup, my monumental-assed grandmother
never turned down a single kolacky from Kransky's Bakery,
or refused a perozhki with cream.
She was too wise to go on a diet
with the whole world starving for love.

BLUE HAIR BLUES

I'm feeling crazy today, because I've poured everything I know into the poems I wrote for twelve year old Monica Poorman from White Horse, South Dakota, who wants more animal poems, and seventy-five year old Sister Alba from St. Catherine's College in St. Paul, Minnesota, who wants more poems about women, and forty year old Dirk Saunders, forester from Boseman, Montana, who wants more tree poems, and fifty year old Dr. Alicia Silversteen, who wants more truth about parents and kids, and twenty-six year old Jay Marakesh, the psychotic who lives at the library and wants only sexy poems, and seventy year old Nancy Hauser, the brilliant dancer and choreographer, who says I've given a lot but please don't stop, and hands me the silver earrings still warm from her ears. I met all these people and more at poetry readings. Only eighty year old Leila Stone from Good Shepherd's Home For The Elderly didn't like my poems. She said she didn't stay alive this long just to sit and hear some silly poet read poems during her lunch hour, no way. When the aide suggested she could wheel herself out of the room if she wanted, she said she would wait for her hair appointment by the door, thank you very much. After an hour she wheeled back in and her hair was so blue she looked as if she'd been to another planet. The aide said, "Leila, you like church music, don't you? Freya's going to read a poem about church music!" When I finished the poem everyone in the room started describing the most meaningful experience they'd ever had in church—but not Leila. She closed her mouth up tight as a cat's ass and shook her head. She waited until I was climbing into my car to careen up in her wheelchair and announce, "I was a terrible wife. Mean to my husband from dawn to dusk. He was a good man, too. Never raised his voice to me or the children. Now he's gone to his Maker and he thinks I'm planning to follow. Well, he's got another think coming!" Guess I'll take a lesson or two from Leila, slam my silver wheelchair into peoples' arms and legs and gobble the mayonnaise off my bread and refuse to agree with anything. Me and Leila could disappear every few days and come back with our hair bluer and bluer. So blue everyone would have to buy sunglasses. So blue the buttons would pop off policemen's shirts and roll into the storm drains underneath the streets of St. Paul. So blue perfectly trained horses would throw off their masters and gallop circles around every town from Montana to Texas. So blue the grass would start singing. So blue God would have to come down and take me and Leila home to his rocking blue sea in the sky, singing those same rude down home Blues he always sings, you know the tune.

LILACS

I'm cutting non-bearing
cherries and grapes
out of the house-high lilacs.
The grape vines, wrist thick,
snare my feet, dart at my eyes,
as I rip them down,
my full weight on each vine.
A pile of dead brush
as wide as a train
winds across our yard,
and the heart-shaped lilacs
reach into space and sun.
"What do you think about
all morning?" Tom asks.

Leaf, stem, branch, trunk,
save the best branches,
cut others away.
Old friends,
conversations,
lovers.
Bend, lift,
drip from every pore.

A botonist arrives
to name some shrubs I can't recall.
"Holy cow!" he whoops,
when he sees the lilac trees.
"Holy cow?" echoes my husband.
"Haven't heard that expression in years!"
The expert falls silent
until he sees the Burning Bush,
large as a garage, "Holy cow!
Wait till fall, when that turns red!"

This land is not mine.
Two sons passed through my body
on their way into the world.
Poems come through me
from underground.
My fingers trace the splinters
of a broken lilac tree
seventy-five years old,
eight inches thick,
its inner rings as violet
as the lilac flowers in spring.
These live beyond us,
belonging to themselves.

GRASS

I lie in bed
with death on my mind,
with abused children, gangs clashing,
guns roaring, forests dying, lakes choking,
and I can feel it:
grass:
shooting up inside the soles of my feet,
tunneling through my knees,
tall and long and lemony,
tangled blades of green
feathering my thighs, soft as lips,
filling my belly,
hissing, rustling, into my heart.
I sit at my desk,
my best self unseen, unspoken,
words of pain and love and praise,
words I owe, dying on the floor,
but the grass grows, the teeming grass grows.
The longer it grows, the thicker it gets,
the thicker it gets the wetter it gets,
the wetter it gets the greener it gets,
the greener it gets the more my heart shines.
The grass flowers into my arms, my fingers,
up through my neck at a speed faster than the sound of it
thrashing and whispering in my throat.
It sprouts from my eyes, my nose, my ears.
With a green groan it replaces my greying hair,
my brain swelling with seeds of grass,
my mind supple, my throat singing.
Even in my despair with aching joints and withered breasts,
my feet twitch all night like roots,
my womb fills with the juice of the grass,
my heart fills with green light laden with green shadow,
    as grass echoes grass.

I expected to lie down and grow old and lose my grip.
I expected to scream and weep and apologize.
I expected to watch my loved ones get sick, go mad, or die.
I expected to fold into the death around me.
But one night as I floated above sleep,
the grass started to grow in my feet,
and it's been growing ever since.
The grass croons, the grass cradles me,
the grass carries me out of myself into the world I hate
and first fell in love with
as a green child.

A BODY HEALS

A body heals
the way a lake heals
in wider and wider circles
when a stone
falls through its skin.
flesh welcomes
earth's remedies—
wind, music, salt and sage,
into the cream of lymph,
into blood frothing like sea foam.
Lilacs and lilies,
wings of moths and sparrows,
the red oak and white oak,
echo with prayers,
    all these
no more solid than we:
skin, muscle, brain and bone:
millions of waves,
and rivers inside the waves,
and stars inside the rivers,
swollen with light
drawn from the eye of the universe
when it first uncoiled
and flung us,
and named us,
to ripen as we dream.

MESSAGE FROM THE RIGHT BRAIN

We don't need your tanks
to patrol our roads,
here
where rolls of breathing hills
deflect the bullets.
Here if something is injured,
we strip naked, sit as near the river
as we can,
and open the palms of our hands
to cup the tears,
the way any leaf does.

> We get along fine without you,
> like your dreams.

When your astronomers wish
to view us wholly, they must
keep their eyes closed
beneath their closed lids.
Nothing here is just itself:
edges blur,
cores of things erupt
and flow over their skins.
All questions rejoin us
as answers,
illuminated by the local ear.

> You take all or nothing
> once you let go
> and fall toward us,
> never by intention.

We know you think we'd all go mad
without you and your grip.

But you can't rule death:
when it comes, we'll hold it
on outstretched tongues,
until it fills us
like any food, or loving gesture.

HEART

I am. I am. I am.

Heart, church bell of the city,
little bald heart,
dear as a faithful husband,
two-fisted heart,
fighting for space and breath,
acorn heart,
mother to a tree;
heart in the middle of the ocean,
pumping the sea's blue music,
earth mover and shaker,
conducting your orchestra of muscles,
mango heart,
rye-bread heart,
heart full of seeds and thick with roots,
source of all my wanderlust,
and my only home
under the roofless sky.

THE LAKE THAT WHISPERS TO ITSELF

Let me tell you something, Mom. I had a dream last night.
It was so secret I can't tell you. So secret I can't remember it.

— Bly Pope, age 4

SPRING

In nature it is...water that sees and water that dreams.
— Gaston Bachelard

Our black cat follows me
down to the boat house.
He can't understand why he isn't welcome.

I want to write alone,
beside the lake that hears my voice
whether or not I speak

where water enters my eyes as bright drops of light
and flows out as black blood
on this page.

Inside the boat house
sunlight reflected off water
writes dappled messages
on the wooden walls.
Or perhaps it's not writing,
but a song,
soft notes cascading
like cathedral bells.
Or maybe it's
a kind of breathing:
in for darkness,
out for light.
Or, it might be
the fleeting touch
of an invisible lover's fingers:
nothing that can be read,
sung,
or breathed,

only felt,
upon the skin we share with day.

I focus my eyes
on a lily by the shore
until the lake behind it
becomes a hazy fabric
of shimmering crescents,
a slithering backdrop,
rocking docks and boats.
The steady rhythm lulls me
until I no longer see the lily,
or the lake.
I no longer see anything,
except myself,
which is surprising,
because I have disappeared.

The far shore
is nearly invisible all winter,
muted by fog or wind-whipped snow,
but now green leaves unfurl
from black twigs and branches
and shape themselves
into round hips and breasts,
cradling homes and gardens.
Unfrozen, the restless lake
streams back and forth
in long grey-blue unravelings,
always traveling beyond this dock,
beyond that shore,
going someplace I cannot go
for now.

A blue heron on a log
pauses in mid-stride,
lowers his s-shaped neck,
and pretends he is a branch
with willow twigs for legs.

Power boats churn past,
fraying the underwater hum,
but the blue heron waits, unmoving,
with hunched shoulders, stony eyes,
and a few wild feathers ruffling on top of his head.

In over an hour no fish swims near,
so the blue heron opens his wings
wider than my arms can reach, and flies away,
his long skinny legs hanging down helplessly
like a workman coming home with no pay.

5

A man and his wife troll past
in their sun-blistered boat.
His left hand curves around the throttle
while his right hand jerks a fishing rod,
the line trapped in underwater weeds.
Her wide, comfortable back
is turned away from him.
She watches her thin line bend to a bite,
pulls up the hook, finds it empty,
and re-baits it, shaking her head.
They do not speak,
their motor puttering across the placid bay
as they circle north, then east,
smaller and smaller,
two vertical lines on a horizontal line,
three brush strokes
suddenly painted out
by the softly swelling lake.

Here on the lake
I am still free
to stand naked
and alone.

Silence flows
from every leaf.
Mist snakes
over the untouched marsh.

This is how it is:
facing the last pocket of true spring,
the condominium-brained city
at my back.

At dusk
thousands of white moths
descend from the trees
and stream
toward the lake.
They flutter
inches above the water
without touching each other.
Like giant snowflakes
in a ground blizzard,
the soft mute moths
dance together
until it's too dark
to see.
So I fall asleep
and dream
a field
of white flower petals
is carrying a black mountain
into the sky.

SUMMER

The swimmer obeys the desire for courage.
— Gaston Bachelard

The first time I dive under water
and open my eyes near shore
I see the glowing brown snails
of Blueberry Lake.
Shaggy mussels too,
that pump themselves shut
when I touch their soft lips.
And old sticks, soggy and twisted,
wriggling like water snakes
through rust-soft, leathery reeds.
And acorns, worn creamy white
in the constant waves, caught
between rocks and pebbles:
pink, brown, green, and blue.
And one grey stone
with the black and white print
of a maple leaf
stamped on it forever
by the press of winter ice.

Thank you for the oval white stone
with a small thumb-sized dent
to hold the sun and rain.

My calloused fingers
smooth its wave-tumbled skin,
and I fling it, high,

and watch it arc,
and drop,
into deep water.

I wait, then,
for the next true stone
to take my hand.

Far off, waves sizzle silver,
but closer, half way across,
they flatten and turn grey,
and then, transparent, still rippling,
soft lip after soft lip,
they crease the palomino sand,
as I lean forward, worn too,
becoming lovely on the shore.

When a loon cries
from the lake's center
I swim out to find him.

No female loon has joined
this yearning, unquenchable male,
who wails all summer with no reply.

His spooky treble
pierces the summer haze,
and spirals into the galaxies of my heart.

Everything's deeper
than I imagined,
mirror clear, and true.

5

I look twenty feet down
into glassy green caves
where bass and walleye hang,
opening and closing their mouths,
but I see no underwater springs,
no sunken trees or docks.
I can't find a reason
why water flows
the way it flows,
beside itself,
into itself,
out of itself,
and away.

When I let myself float,
some invisible presence pulls me
toward the deepest part of the lake.
In the shrouded bottom,
I picture walleye and turtles
feeding on shrimp-shaped Daphnia.
Soon they are joined
by supernatural creatures,
looming under my soft belly
as real as visions or nightmares.
I am bathed by liquid paws,
rocked by demons,
sung to by angels:
scattered, suspended,
like salt in the sea.

A door opens in the water,

a silver rectangle
slanting down.

It beckons,
in the vast, grey waves.

I want to swim over
and dive through.

But what if it closes
behind me?

How long can I hold
my breath?

In the bay, the water is black
as yesterday's nightmare.
Ebony roots stretch down
toward a murky bottom.
A black snake parts the waves.
A giant carp, half the length of my body,
looms toward me, and disappears.
Soon something more dangerous will emerge,
something too much for me to bear.

Water echoes
what it touches:
a boat,
        a dock,
                a lily pad,
repeating the fluid syllables
over and over,
until it ebbs free,
and rides,
        wordless,
                to its edge,
or back to some immaculate center,
a place I cannot know.

If I die in water
my body will sink
through a string of silver bubbles
        rising toward the surface
                from between my lips

and I will lie on the bottom
while fish mouth
my mute flesh.

Floating in the lake,
cradled by water,
how is it possible
I feel nothing
about my father's death?

After he died
I devoted myself to water,
where my image,
forever doubled,
dies every minute.

Waves caress my body
as they would a stone,
until, at last, the lake enters,
and the dead one
comes out in my tears.

When you died, father,
you gave me a perfect grief.
I cradle it on my chest
like a heavy fieldstone.
It protects me,
and carries me to the bottom of the lake
when I jump in.
Deep in mud, I let go,
and rise to the surface
with a face full of light.
Thank you, father,
for this perfect grief.

∽

Beyond grief: the sun and moon
kindle gold fires on the lake,
which stream off to distant inlets
and return, relit, in every color.
Waves rise in ridges and furrows,
driven from beneath by humpbacked creatures,
somersaulting north and south, then east and west,
blurring blue over grey, or, on humid days,
every dancing shade of green.
Once, elegant women with parasols
slipped down to the shore to be rowed to and fro
by men with hats pushed back from their pale foreheads,
while other women scrubbed clothes on the rocks
and watched their laughing, bronzed children
leap from cliffs into the water;
and now, sailboats unfurl and flutter
like moths against the wind,
and fierce motorboats pull flying acrobats on skis.
All this the lake will bear,
and still return each spring
from blocks of ice and salt
as tears.

When I was four I learned how water
embraces all of me at once,
how it is both hard and soft:
more earth than air,
more moonlight than moon.

After I fell in love with water
I never woke wondering who I was
or what to do. I swam,
and watched the skin of the lake
endlessly replace itself.

I would say water
is my mother,
but since I am a mother
I know how much I fall short
of what water gives.

I teach my children to swim:
"Immerse your slender wrists,
their blue rivers of blood,
in the sun-warmed water
lapping clear above the yellow sand.
Sit, and feel the silken-fresh romp of waves
along your legs and chest.
Lie down and drift into deeper water,
noting how every out-breath
tells you when to close your mouth,
and only briefly drops you deeper:
and how every in-breath supports you
until you bob up, safe and smiling.
Let your hands flutter like fins
and your feet flail like rudders,
and you've done it.
You're more than who you were on shore,
swimming in God's tears,
almost as nimble and clever as fish,
surely as droll and tender as frogs.
Dear children, believe me,
you may trust the water
as you would a caring friend,
if you accept one more truth
about the gift of swimming:
always *be afraid*."

My children, my little fish,
soar to the surface
seeking green fire.

I panic as they slip worms and water bugs
between their lips
and two-faced silver hooks.

Some take the bait again and again
until they're too big to be thrown back
and are readied for the feast,
beautifully open to the knife.

My claws and wits erode
in the dark and heavy tide
that erases me, echoes me.

I'm a mother creature.
I let smaller creatures go.
I let them go.

A cool wind
braids
the lake's long hair.
Rivers of darkness
weave through
rivers of light.
Black cloud footprints
walk the sun-whitened water.
It would be better
to be a painter
than a writer.
No, it would be better
to be a swimmer,
stroking out to meet my lover.
No. It would be best of all
to stop swimming, and drown,
and live forever
in the lake's long hair

FALL

The past life of the soul is itself a deep water.
— Gaston Bachelard

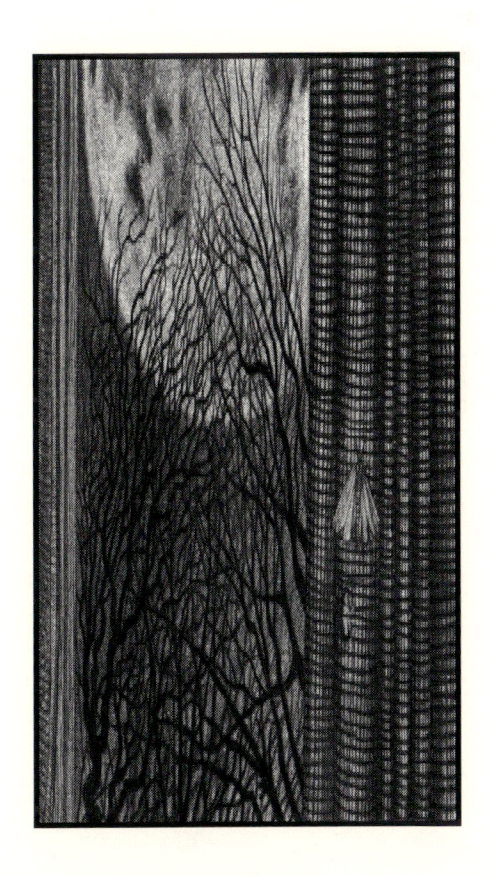

Every morning I walk down the hill to write
in the rotting boat house by the lake,
more at home than I have been anywhere
since the summer I learned to swim.
Water lips against the dock,
as it did in early June, when I began.
A few sugar bees hover among dry lily stalks.
Two chipmunks chase past the door,
thumping their black feet on the wooden deck.
One of them turns and stares at me,
while I gape at him, in my old woolen hat.
I am speechless, but he is not.

What he says will be my next poem.

How I have neglected you, lake.
So many days and nights I could have
come and watched you
or better yet, waded in,
and let you drum upon my heart.
What was I doing? Cooking?
Cleaning house? Worrying about money?
I can't find words
to describe your sound today.
Smooth? Round? Arriving? Departing?
No, none of these, and all of them,
with boundless silences between.
Both where you ought to be
and where you are.

When the wind swaggers in from the north
I hear waves all night,
beating fat against the shore,
a sturdier sound than the ghosty wail of trees.
Even when the wind whines or gusts,
water's reply is a reassuring thump,
measured and certain.

Water serves each moment equally,
never frightening me with howling
harp-like voices in the dark.
Living beside water's bass and drums
I improvise all day like a flute or violin;
and when I'm weary, worn thin by blustery life,
water leads me down its broad safe steps to sleep.

Two steel grey salmon
leap in the sun along the shore.
I snorkle out to look at them,
but when my black shadow falls,
they jet in opposite directions,
to meet again, in secret, under waterweed.
I am permitted to glimpse, for one second,
their round, fingernail-sized, overlapping scales,
their perfect, boat-shaped bodies,
their grim, determined mouths.
Transplanted from Lake Superior
their world has shrunk
to this small suburban lake
where they can't reproduce.
Fishermen will catch them,
or they'll die under the ice this winter.
But now, they rise from the waves,
belly to belly, heart to heart,
into the open, into light,
dark travelers.

Waves slosh and bubble
like soapy green dishwater.
Brown islands of uprooted lakeweed
tangle with sodden black logs,
and rotting, bloated fish.
I dive deeper, into water
streaked with golden legs of sun,
down, down,
into one clear tear drop
in a heart-shaped hollow of sand.

I don't believe it, but it's true.

S

It wasn't safe to swim today.
White breakers stampeding south
were only slightly warmer than the sky.
Black water bled up from the bottom
in ominous thunder heads
I forced myself to cross.
With every stroke I gasped for air,
staying near shore in case I needed help.

I swam for three reasons:

I wanted to see the sunfish one last time.

I didn't want to face my poems.

And I was angry
with the man who laughed
when I asked him to keep an eye out
while I swam,
the romantic who believes,
as he did when we first met,
that I'm too good a swimmer
to drown.

A giant black wing
lies curved across the silver lake,
stretching from one end to the other.

It appeared suddenly,
as if it had risen out of the water,
or fallen from the sky.

A lake sometimes turns toward itself
in small precise gestures
along hidden shoals, or sandbars.

I never saw water take the shape of a black wing,
but that is what I see tonight,
waiting on the shore.

From my frosted window
I see the black outline of the boat house
where I've had so little time to write.

The wind rises as the temperature drops.
Cicadas ride waves of song
toward the dark earth and setting sun.

Honking ducks land on the lake
and bob up and down
under a half moon.

The ducks call out
guttural blessings
to each other:

"We have come this far."
"We have so far to go."

WINTER

Water is the blood of the earth.
— Gaston Bachelard

Summer's over.
No more rocking in the waves,
clear water skin sliding between me and the sky.
No floating, chin up, down the silky path
the sun makes across the lake at dusk.
No dropping to the bottom, naked,
in the chocolate midnight.
Poor fish, stuck inside the house all winter.
Poor, dry, bloodless, soulless thing.

Once a week I trudge down to the lake
through knee-deep snowdrifts.
I creep across the moon-scarred ice,
glowing in the afternoon twilight
like the underbelly of a dead fish.
On shore our neighbors' houses
drift among the frozen white hills
like abandoned ships.
Under the ice, creatures I cannot see
devour smaller, weaker creatures.
I'm alone, without visions,
on the deserted lake—
the fierce, blinding mirror
of winter.

Down on the frozen lake,
I look for signs of life.
In the center of the bay
I find three round holes
drilled and abandoned by ice fishermen.
I lie on my stomach and peer
into one pale green cylinder,
hoping a fish will swim by.
I wait until the entire lake
tilts upright—with me at the knothole—
but I see no fish, no mermaids, no stars,
just pure water rising toward me
from a meadow of green light:

like a memory of a dream
of a place I once
belonged.

Grief has crept upon me lately, and not so lately,
from the black undersides of fallen leaves
and the empty spaces between the crumbs of my bread

until I cannot care about anyone or anything
with the passion I once cherished.
I am able to love small things only.

Out on this lake patches of silver dance,
sun on ice,
tiny seeds of light

which become black holes
leading into the universe
that lies behind all things.

5

Slabs of ice blown by a stiff southern wind
scale off the water, and hit shore.
Under the wildly glistening newborn waves
I count dead fish and frogs
belly up on the lake bottom.
My poems and I have died
a thousand deaths this winter.

5

I lie on the dock
and peer through the boards,
my body warm for the first time since last September.
Underneath me the water lies still
over the sandy bottom
like the sky above the distant hills,
clear and weightless
as sleep.

The only poem I know
is the one sleep uncovers
in the lake that flows under me,
the lake I will die next to
that cannot die itself.

I drop naked, with faith, into darkness,
and my eyes look tenderly
into transparent water eyes,
and the only poem I know
comes

to meet itself in me.

❡ ACKNOWLEDGMENTS

I am grateful to the editors of the following publications for poems or versions of poems which originally appeared in them: *The American Poetry Review; American Poets Anthology: published in China; 1984 Anthology of Verse and Yearbook of American Poetry; The Boundaries of Twilight, Anthology of Czecho-Slovak Writing From The New World, New Rivers Press; Leaning Into The Wind, Anthology, Houghton-Mifflin; Eve's Legacy...Adam's Apple; High Plains Literary Review; Mankato Poetry Review; Lake Country Journal; Michigan Quarterly Review; The Midwest Quarterly; Mothering, The Magazine Of Natural Family Living; New Zoo Poetry Review; The North Coast Review; The North Stone Review; Orphic Lute; The Pacific Review; Poems Of The Great Lakes: Milkweed Editions; Poetry Harbor; Poetry Now; Essential Love: Poetworks/Grayson Books; Proposing On the Brooklyn Bridge: Poetworks/Grayson Books; Radcliffe Quarterly; Redstart; Red Weather: North Dakota Anthology; Rhino; The Shining Times; South Dakota Review; Spirit Horse Press; Voices and Visions: Bunting Institute Anthology, Harvard Press; The Western Journal Of Medicine; Windfall Prophets Press; The Wolf Head Quarterly; Writing The Dakotas, Nine Contemporary Poets: The South Dakota Review; Yankee.*

The following poems appeared in *FLESH AND BLOOD*, a chapbook from Red Dragonfly Press, December 2000, Ed. Scott King. *Giving Birth, A Body Heals, Heart, Message From The Right Brain, Ear, Men's Tears, Hair, Toes, Asses, My Grandmother's Ass, The Husband Speaks Of Menopause, The Wife Speaks of Menopause*, and *Tom*.

The illustrations used in this book were originally published in *Dark Fire* (2003) — poems by Bly Pope & artwork by Bly Pope and Rowan Pope.